THE LOCH NESS MONSTER

JEN BESEL

BLACK RABBIT BOOKS

Bolt Jr. is published by Black Rabbit Books
P.O. Box 3263, Mankato, Minnesota, 56002.
www.blackrabbitbooks.com
Copyright © 2020 Black Rabbit Books

Grant Gould, designer; Omay Ayres, photo researcher

Names: Besel, Jennifer M., author.
Title: The Loch Ness monster / by Jen Besel.
Description: Mankato, MN : Black Rabbit Books, 2020.
Series: Bolt Jr. a little bit spooky | Audience: Age 6-8. |
Audience: K to Grade 3. | Includes bibliographical references
and index. Identifiers: LCCN 2019001490 (print) |
LCCN 2019011252 (ebook) | ISBN 9781623101855 (ebook)
| ISBN 9781623101794 (library binding) |
ISBN 9781644661178 (paperback)
Subjects: LCSH: Loch Ness monster—Juvenile literature.
Classification: LCC QL89.2.L6 (ebook) | LCC QL89.2.L6 B48
2020 (print) | DDC 001.944—dc23
LC record available at https://lccn.loc.gov/2019001490

Printed in the United States. 5/19

Image Credits
Alamy: Chronicle, 12; Dreamstime: Fernando Gregory, 10–11;
imgur.com: Simon Stalenhag, 22–23; maps.apple.com: Apple
Maps, 17 (bkgd); Science Source: Chris Butler, Cover; Shutterstock:
Bob Orsillo, 8–9, 20–21; Fer Gregory, 16-17 (monster);
Lubomira08, 5; MicroOne, 3, 24; Ralf Juergen Kraft, 10; Rich
Carey, 7, 20–21; Vector Icon Flat, 14 (map); Victor Habbick, 18–19;
Warpaint, 1, 4, 13, 14 (bkgd); twitter.com: Mark Witton, 6–7

Contents

CHAPTER 1

A Scary Sight

Two people drove around **Loch** Ness. Suddenly, they saw a black **creature** in the water. It made huge waves. Was it the Loch Ness monster?

loch: a lake

creature: a strange being

Loch Ness monster

stories say at least ◀ · · · · · · · **LENGTH COMPARISON** ·
20 feet
(6 meters)

A Big Mystery

Loch Ness is a deep, dark lake. Many people say they've seen a monster there. They say it has smooth skin. It also has a long tail. People have searched. But no one has answers.

whale shark
18 to 33 feet
(5 to 10 m)

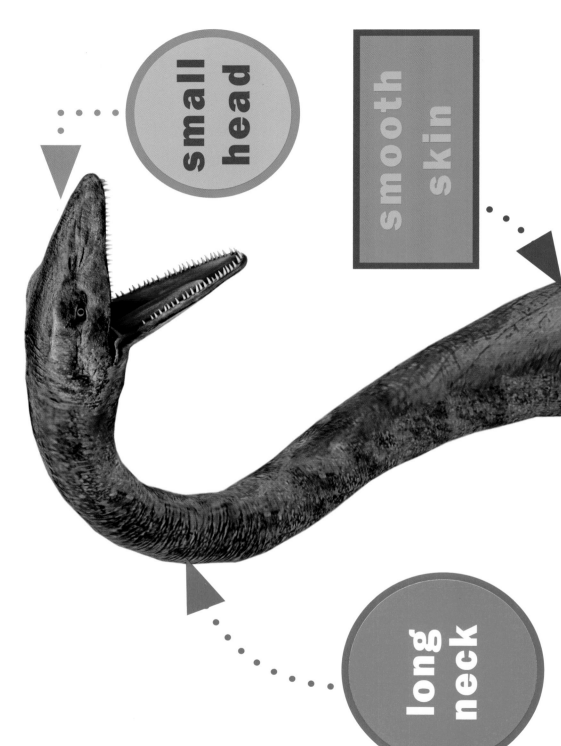

LOCH NESS

Monster Features

small head

smooth skin

long neck

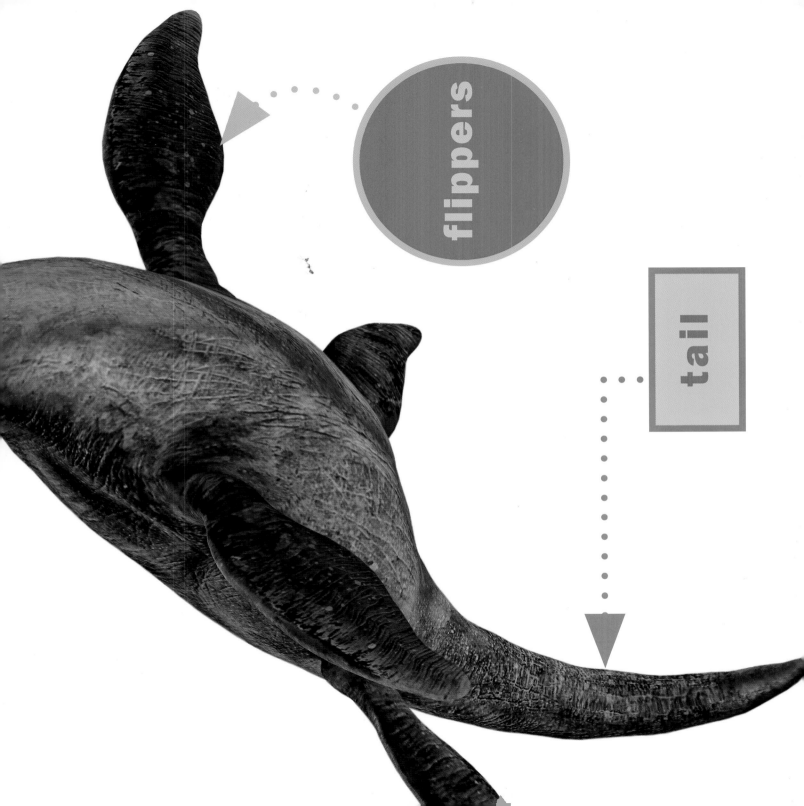

flippers

tail

CHAPTER 2

Monster Stories

People have many stories about the lake monster. It even has a **nickname**. Many call it Nessie. Stories say Nessie is huge. It also has humps.

nickname: a name other than the real name

FACT

Some think Nessie is a dinosaur.

11

Pictures

Some people have tried to take pictures of Nessie. Most pictures are **blurry**. Others are from far away. No one has a good picture.

blurry: not clear

WHERE IS
Loch Ness?

Europe

Scotland

KEY

= Loch Ness

CHAPTER 3

Finding Answers

Researchers study the lake. They use tools that find underwater objects. The tools have found big animals. Some people think that was Nessie.

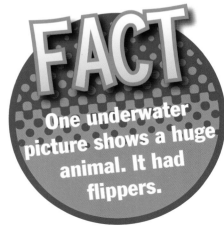

FACT

One underwater picture shows a huge animal. It had flippers.

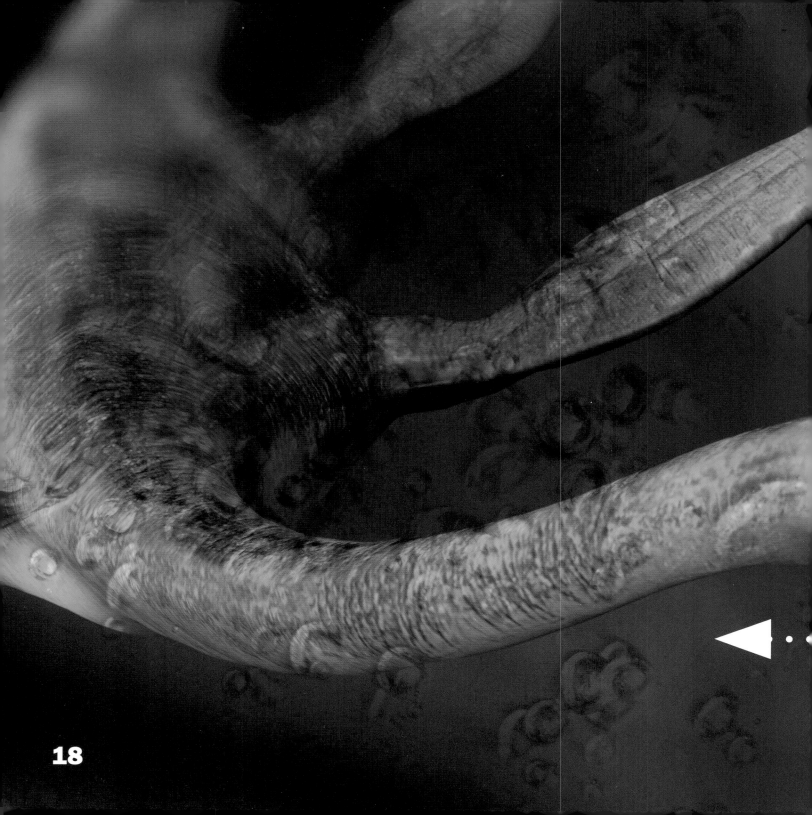

18

Hard to Explain

Some people think Nessie is something normal. It could be a big fish. Maybe it's a seal. But others still believe it's a monster. What do you think?

**Depth of Loch Ness
up to 754 feet
(230 m)**

Bonus Facts

People have told Nessie stories for at least 1,500 years.

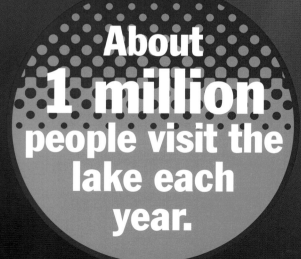

About **1 million** people visit the lake each year.

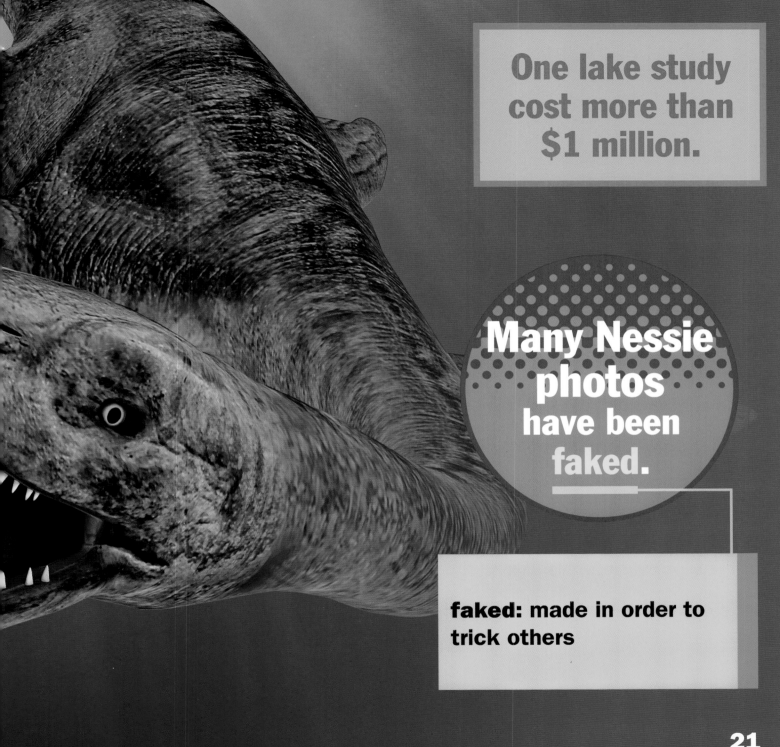

One lake study cost more than $1 million.

Many Nessie photos have been faked.

faked: made in order to trick others

READ MORE/WEBSITES

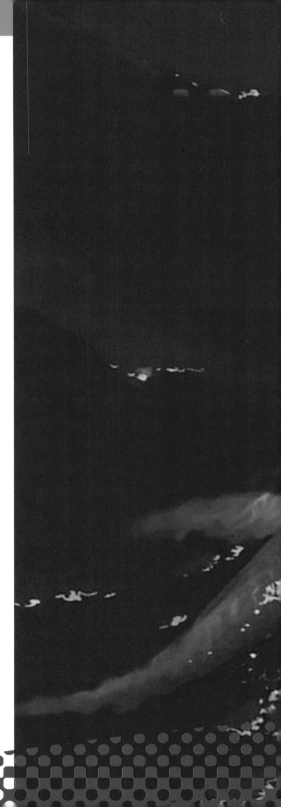

Don, Lari. *The Treasure of the Loch Ness Monster.* Picture Kelpies: Traditional Scottish Tales. Edinburgh: Kelpies, 2018.

Murray, Laura K. *Loch Ness Monster.* Are They Real? Mankato, MN: Creative Education/Creative Paperbacks, 2017.

Oachs, Emily Rose. *The Loch Ness Monster.* Investigating the Unexplained. Minneapolis: Bellwether Media, Inc., 2019.

Loch Ness Monster Facts for Kids
kids.kiddle.co/Loch_Ness_Monster

Loch Ness Monster Hoax
video.nationalgeographic.com/video/loch-ness-sci

Nessie–the Loch Ness Monster
learnenglishkids.britishcouncil.org/en/short-stories/nessie-the-loch-ness-monster

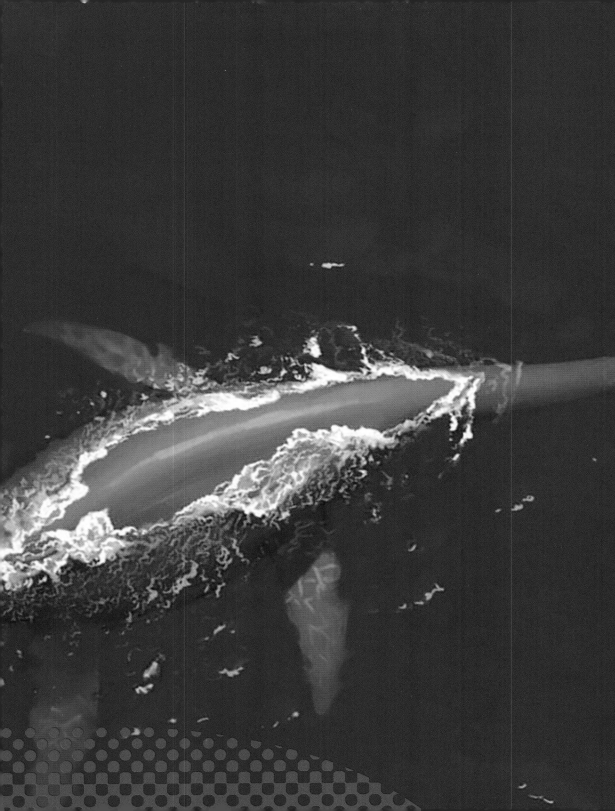

GLOSSARY

blurry (BLUR-ee)—not clear

creature (KREE-chur)—a strange being

faked (FAYKD)—made in order to trick others

loch (LAHK)—a lake

nickname (NIK-naym)—a name other than the real name

INDEX